KU-067-083

COMMUNICATING BETTER WITH PEOPLE ON THE AUTISM SPECTRUM

35 THINGS
YOU NEED TO KNOW

LLYFRGELL WREO>AM
RARY SERVICE

35

PADDY-JOE MORAN

Jessica Kingsley *Publishers*
London and Philadelphia

First published in 2016
by Jessica Kingsley Publishers
73 Collier Street
London N1 9BE, UK
and
400 Market Street, Suite 400
Philadelphia, PA 19106, USA

www.jkp.com

Copyright © Paddy-Joe Moran 2016

All rights reserved. No part of this publication may be reproduced in any material form
(including photocopying, storing in any medium by electronic means or transmitting)
without the written permission of the copyright owner except in accordance with the
provisions of the law or under terms of a licence issued in the UK by the Copyright
Licensing Agency Ltd. www.cla.co.uk or in overseas territories by the relevant
reproduction rights organisation, for details see www.ifrro.org. Applications for the
copyright owner's written permission to reproduce any part of this publication should be
addressed to the publisher.

Warning: The doing of an unauthorised act in relation to a copyright work may result in
both a civil claim for damages and criminal prosecution.

Library of Congress Cataloging in Publication Data
Title: Communicating better with people on the autism spectrum : 35 things
   you need to know / Paddy-Joe Moran.
Description: London ; Philadelphia : Jessica Kingsley Publishers, 2016.
Identifiers: LCCN 2016010283 | ISBN 9781849057080 (alk. paper)
Subjects: LCSH: Autism. | Autistic people--Language. | Autistic
   people--Rehabilitation.
Classification: LCC RC553.A88 M6772 2016 | DDC 616.85/882--dc23 LC
record available at https://urldefense.proofpoint.com/v2/url?u=https-3A__lccn.
loc.gov_2016010283&d=BQIFAg&c=euGZstcaTDllvimEN8b7jXrwqOf-
v5A_CdpgnVftiiMM&r=VCKr2NBFNTs4O_kp07esGY2J-doQEb4zTq5sCaeXa-
I&m=U104C_gBEm0YoEPkH-FLcbrUlm3ibNK_AjZlkWmI1-E&s=hcrcCLmpGFPxw
8fYscWqL1R07RvRgUWEDEbRVrPDwLE&e=

British Library Cataloguing in Publication Data
A CIP catalogue record for this book is available from the British Library

ISBN 978 1 84905 708 0
eISBN 978 1 78450 234 8

Printed and bound in Great Britain

MIX
Paper from
responsible sources
FSC
www.fsc.org   FSC® C013056

WREXHAM C.B.C LIBRARY	
LLYFRGELL B.S. WRECSAM	
C56 0000 0634 097	
Askews & Holts	20-Dec-2016
616.85882	£7.99
	WXMWREXHAM

In loving memory of my Grandma Winifred McDowell
March 1934 to May 2015

CONTENTS

Introduction   7

1. Person-first Language – to Use It or Not?   **12**
2. Use Non-patronising Language   **15**
3. Use Age-appropriate Language   **18**
4. Use Neutral Language   **20**
5. Let Yourself Be Guided on
    Preferred Terminology   **23**
6. Don't Use the Word 'Normal'   **27**
7. There Is Nothing 'Mild' About
    Asperger's Syndrome   **29**
8. Say 'On the Spectrum'   **32**
9. Address the Person Directly   **33**
10. Refer to Parents by Name   **35**
11. Adapting Your Language and
    the Way You Speak   **37**
12. You Will Be Taken Literally   **39**
13. Sarcasm   **41**
14. The Use of Functioning Labels   **43**
15. Non-verbal vs Pre-verbal   **47**

16.	Pre-conceived Ideas	49
17.	Appearances Can Be Deceptive	51
18.	Triad of Impairments	55
19.	Giftedness Is Not a Given	57
20.	Autism Is a Neurological Condition	60
21.	Autistic Person, Not Patient	63
22.	No Need to Grieve	65
23.	Puzzling	67
24.	Facial Expressions	69
25.	Body Language	71
26.	Environment	73
27.	Physical Contact	75
28.	Have a Time Limit on the Session	77
29.	Offer Breaks During Sessions	79
30.	Explain What Will Be Happening, and When	82
31.	Stick to the Plan	84
32.	Ask Specific Rather than Open-ended Questions	86
33.	Pace Your Speech	88
34.	Alternatives to Non-verbal Communication	90
35.	Things to Consider When Offering Food	92

| *Conclusion* | 94 |

INTRODUCTION

Over the years I have come into contact with numerous health and social care professionals, and I have to say my experiences with them have been mixed. As a young man with autism I can look back at some of the interactions I had with professionals when I was a child, and see that they have helped me tremendously. I was eight when I was first diagnosed with autism, and the years after that were packed full of meetings and assessments. It was a case of having to go here, there and everywhere to try and get the services I needed. There were huge waiting lists, and hours upon hours of phone calls even to get to a meeting. We would meet with people to talk about one issue, who would then recommend we talk to someone else about another issue, and so on. This is something that most people with autism and their families have to put up with – especially in the first few years after a diagnosis. I am sure it will be a familiar picture to a lot of families. Some of the issues I was dealing with at that time were sadly beyond what my family and I could deal with on our own. I stress this point so early on as I believe I have to make clear at the start of this book that my aim is not to insult or imply any lack of professionalism in my readers.

As I have said, when I look back to being a young child and being helped along by professionals working in tandem with my family, I know that what was done for me played a big part in me even being able to write a book like this. I was at a stage where I found it all but impossible to sleep in my own bed. I would have outbursts and meltdowns at the change from weekdays to weekend, for example, and I would feel physically ill every day with stress. Daily outbursts and lack of sleep were taking a massive toll on me. I found it harder and harder to get by in day-to-day life. As a family we managed to tackle a lot of the issues ourselves, but still when we got to meet professionals, and found out just how helpful they could be, it was a huge relief to us all. My family played a huge part in helping me to deal with these issues, but I do also have to give credit where credit is due to the professionals who worked with me.

But it has been a mixed set of interactions. If I think back over the past 12 months I can pick out three times I have had to deal with an autism professional who just did not get it. Now I am not saying that they were vindictive, or anything like that – they just did not seem to understand the basics. When I look at the professionals I have dealt with this past year I cannot credit them with anything other than increasing my stress levels. I have had an appointment that overran by nearly two hours, I have seen professionals who did not understand that autism is not a mental health issue, and I have had three appointments that were needlessly long and gruelling.

One appointment was aimed at seeing what help I would need for university. I went into it quite happy, and more than willing to do what needed to be done to get the help I required. When I came out I was so stressed I could not calm down for days. Now in all fairness I got a lot of help during my time at university as a result of that meeting, but to tell the truth, when I was in there, and in the days and even weeks after, it did not feel worth it. In fact, I almost got to the point of saying I did not want to go to university after all if that was any indication of what life would be like. In the end, I did go, and the stress of the meeting faded. But even looking back now I can see how poorly that meeting, and other meetings that followed, were set up.

As much as it might sound like it, this book is not being written simply for me to vent my feelings. The main aim I have in writing it is to try and help professionals get to grips with some basic, and easy to implement tips for dealing with us autistic people. Because I do understand that sometimes for an outsider looking in, no matter what qualifications you may have, we can be a bit hard to understand. The tips in this book are not just things I have thought up that would help me – they are things a lot of autistic people talk about. These are concerns most people with autism will have, but might not be able to communicate. So I hope that this book proves useful to you, and can help you in your interactions with autistic people in the future.

The truth about language is that it is always changing, and what is okay to say one day is often viewed as offensive and wrong the next. But that's okay – people, especially those who work as professionals interacting daily with those directly affected by the words they use, need to be able to change with the times. It's no use saying 'when I got my degree we could say that'. Or 'in all the books I studied this phrase was used'. That was then, and this is now. I have to admit that in my past writing I used phrases that at the time were viewed as fine, but now I do not like, and wish I could remove from my work – such as the term 'Triad of Impairments' in my first book. But there it is, I can't change the past any more than the reader of this book can. But having used a word or phrase once does not mean that it is now stuck in your vocabulary, and cannot be expunged. There is no need to feel bad if you have done anything this book advises you not to do, or if you have not done something it says you should. That's not the point of the book at all. The point of the book is to give voice to all the things autistic people want you to know about the language used around autism when we go into meetings and appointments with you. Chapters 24–35 deal with non-language-based tips. They are no less important, and can all have a positive and profound impact. It is well known that autistic people can struggle with non-verbal communication, and some of the tips here can help with that. Others will look at the impact the room you talk in itself can have, and so on. As with the points in the first half of the book, these are not intended to attack anything you might be doing as a professional, but rather, they are meant to give you positive advice on things you could do in order to improve the way you work. You might have got things wrong in the past, but so has everyone. There is nothing wrong with that. It's not about looking back at what you might have said, rather it's about taking a look at what autistic people want you to know, and thinking about what you can do and change going forward to help the people you work with, and also yourself.

Language is powerful and the words you use have a long-term impact on autistic people, and on how they feel about themselves. You need to think about this before you speak.

#1

PERSON-FIRST LANGUAGE – TO USE IT OR NOT?

What is person-first language and should professionals use it or not? Some people believe that by saying someone is an 'autistic person' this is placing the autism before the person, as if you are in some way saying that the autism is the biggest part of them, their sole defining feature. So person-first language is just what it sounds like: instead of saying 'autistic person' you would say 'person with autism'. However, many people with autism are more than happy to be called 'autistic' as they believe their autism is such a big part of them that it does effectively define them, and they are fine with this. Feelings on whether or not to use person-first language can run high, and it is a divisive issue in the autism community. Issues can arise due to the fact that a lot of parents are fans of person-first language, whereas most autistic people like to be called autistic rather than a person with autism. This will not be true in all cases, but it is something to think about. The professional's job is to make the autistic person happy, not their parents. If a professional talks to someone with autism in a way they find to be demeaning, then it will have a negative impact on that meeting and on all further meetings between that professional and the autistic person.

Many people on the autism spectrum use both terms interchangeably, without issue, and would be happy for professionals to do so. But it is important for professionals to make an effort to find out what the autistic person prefers before they start using either of the phrases. What you need to do is to put aside any feelings you have about what type of language should be used, and just ask the person you are working with. Whatever they decide, try and stick to it. You might be a strong believer in the use of person-first language, but if you are working with someone who feels the opposite then it's not up to you to try and convince them, rather just to put them at ease. Adjust what you do, and the way you speak, to benefit whomever you are working with at the time. Of course you may run into issues if the autistic person finds it hard to communicate their preference to you, or is non-verbal. However, they might be able to write something down, or just show you some sign in their own way. Listening to what the autistic person is saying is key to making sure things go well.

Try and refer to the person by their name as often as you can, not just when talking to them face to face, but in notes and on forms as well. You will not be able to avoid the issue of whether to use person-first language forever by doing this – and nor would you want to – it's not that big a deal after all if you just find out which the person prefers, and stick to it.

#2

....

USE NON-PATRONISING LANGUAGE

One of the worst things professionals can do when talking to someone with autism is to patronise them. Patronising language can take several forms, such as overexplaining, oversimplifying or pretending to take somebody seriously. This can have a demeaning effect on those being spoken to. It shows a deep lack of respect, and also sets the professional up as being someone who is looking down on the autistic person, as if they are viewing them from the outside rather than being someone they can work with. A lot of the time this is not done through malice: a professional will often feel that part of their job is to do and say what's best for the autistic individual, and in their mind part of this might involve using language to try and soften what they say. This is intended to shelter and protect the autistic person, but this does not mean it is helpful.

So what can you do to avoid this?

Explain as much as is needed. Do not feel as if you have to go into a massive amount of detail about any and every thing you ask the autistic person to do. They may well not understand your first explanation, and that's okay – you can go back over things, and explain more. This is better than assuming every autistic person will find it hard to understand your explanations. In fact, too much information in one go can be overwhelming to people with autism, and they can end up not taking any of it in. They need time to process what is being said to them.

Gauge the level of understanding. Try not to oversimplify things. Some people with autism have a great understanding of what is going on and what is being said, even if they don't look like they are taking things in. It's okay to try and talk about or explain something that is a bit complex to an autistic person – they will either get it or not – but you should at least try to talk to them about it. Making things too simple can just come across as plain rude. Try to work out the individual's level of understanding, instead of just going for the super-simple way of talking from the start.

Judge each issue on its own merits. Nodding and smiling as someone talks about an issue, while at the same time disregarding it in your own mind, is just about one of the most patronising things a professional can do. This might be a case where someone with autism is talking about something they feel might help them and you don't think it will, or it might be someone explaining why they are anxious about something you don't think they should be worried about. But that's the thing: if it means something to them, and if they take it seriously, then you need to as well. And if you just can't, then you need to tell the truth and admit you feel this way. Parents will often nod along and smile at toddlers when they are saying something silly or uninteresting, but this is not something that should ever happen between a professional and an autistic individual.

#3

....

USE AGE-APPROPRIATE LANGUAGE

It is essential to use age-appropriate language when speaking to autistic people. This means that when talking to adults you make sure you avoid the use of childlike language. The use of childlike language is similar to that of patronising language, but in this case I am referring to using childlike names for things such as parts of the body, or animals. Again, it sounds as if you are not taking the person you are talking to seriously, and also it can appear as if you do not respect their intellect. Think about age, but don't get hung up on it; think about the age of whomever you are talking to. If you're talking to an adult, then talk to them the same way you would any other adult. If you notice they are not understanding things, you can simplify some of your language. This does not mean talking to them like you would talk to a baby or young child. In fact, the first thing you might do is to take the time to explain what you mean, and see if they understand after this. It may just be that you were talking too fast, or too loudly for them to follow, rather than them lacking an understanding of what it is you are talking about.

But what about young children? Well, you will have to take into account their age, but at the same time you should not feel the need to talk to them in a way you would not talk to any other child of the same age. Saying all of this, you can't let yourself get hung up too much on age: it is true that some young autistic people can understand far more than others of the same age, whereas some adults with autism do find it hard to understand what is being said to them. But talking to the person in a way that befits their age is a good way to start. You can change and adapt from there.

#4

······································

USE NEUTRAL
LANGUAGE

The language you use as a professional can be key in shaping how autistic people feel after a meeting with you. If your language is negative and downbeat, then what are people meant to draw from this? You may come across as looking like you are negative about autism as a whole, and this can affect the autistic person in many ways. First of all, it can make them feel bad about themselves, as if there is something wrong with them, or that they should be upset, and despondent about having autism. But it can also create a gap between autistic people and the professionals who work with them. Most autistic people are not negative about their autism, and if you are then this will affect your working relationship with them. Also, it can affect how their families view the person's autism. If you diagnose a child, and then make out to the family that autism is a wholly negative thing, not only will you upset them, but you will send them away with a misguided view of autism.

Negative language can include terms such as 'suffers from autism', or any reference to autism as a disease or epidemic. So this is not about raising the real and pressing issues that can come with autism such as outbursts/meltdowns, sensory and emotional overload or having a hard time interacting with others, it is about making autism itself out to be negative as a whole. When diagnosing, be truthful but not negative; telling people about all the issues and troubles they might encounter with autism is fine, but make sure that's not all you talk about. The best professionals talk about both the bad and the good aspects of living with autism. You don't need to make out that being diagnosed is a great thing, as long as you don't make it out to be a bad thing. You can tell newly diagnosed people about autism in stages. So maybe mix it up; have a plan of what you are going to talk about and how you are going to approach it; for example, for each negative point you raise, match it with a positive one.

Let people know they don't 'suffer' from autism. I have highlighted how you can have a bad impact on someone's state of mind if you use negative language, but let's look at the other side of this. Positive language can have a huge impact too – both on people who are newly diagnosed and those who have known about their autism for years. If you explain to them that while autism is a part of them, and a large part of who they are, they don't 'suffer' from it, you can do a lot to help. When you think about it, if someone with autism gets the idea that even professionals who are meant to be experts on autism think he or she is suffering, it must be hard to keep up a positive or neutral outlook. But if you are neutral about autism, pointing out positives as well as negatives, then you can help them realise that autism is not all about suffering and hardship – you can really help to give the autistic person self-confidence, and improve their state of mind. The language used by professionals can have a huge impact on autistic people and their families, so making sure it stays neutral and does not become wholly negative is vital.

#5

....

LET YOURSELF BE GUIDED ON PREFERRED TERMINOLOGY

Disabled, special needs, learning difficulty?

One of the key points that will be reiterated many times in this book is that professionals need to let themselves be guided by the people they are working with. Depending on whom you ask, all three of the terms above are not only acceptable, but also wholly accurate for describing some people with autism. But just because a term or phrase is loved and used by some does not mean everyone in the autistic community is behind it. In fact, all of the above phrases can and will draw a negative reaction from some autistic individuals. Let's take a look at each term separately, starting with what has proven to be the most controversial.

Disabled. This book is not going to wade into the debate about whether autism is a disability or not. This is not the point of the book. The point is to give advice on whether or not you should be using the terms 'disability' or 'disabled' when referring to someone with autism. A good number of autistic people are happy to identify as disabled; they feel that their autism makes everyday tasks so hard that they should be thought of as disabled. Autism is known as a developmental disability, but not a learning disability. So officially it is a disability, and therefore it is okay use the term 'disabled' to describe autistic individuals. But the thing is, a large number of people with autism hate the term. They claim that they are different, but that this makes them no less able than others. Now in reality, the dictionary definition of autism should not dictate whether or not you call autistic people disabled. If someone is clear about the fact that they don't want to be referred to as disabled, then it's only fair to respect this. There is no shame in being referred to as disabled, but at the same time there is a level of respect that should apply when it comes to professionals and the people they work with. Part of that respect means that professionals should not try and enforce their view of autism on autistic people. But this does go both ways: some people with autism are happy to be called disabled. In this case, once again it is okay for the professional to use whatever term the autistic person is most happy with.

Special needs. The term 'special needs' is widely used to refer to people with autism, and much like the word 'disability', it can be very divisive. There are those who see it as a harmless phrase, and are quite happy to use it to describe themselves, believing that the extra help they might require when it comes to their need for routine or their difficulties with social skills would qualify them as having special needs. Now this is fair, and there is nothing wrong with people using the term to describe themselves, but it's like everything else – if you're going to use it in a professional capacity then you should check first. The term 'disability' is often thought to be offensive, whereas 'special needs' is more often thought of as patronising by those who do not like it. The truth is, it does not matter why someone is not fond of a term – it's up to them to dictate whether or not they want someone who is working with them to use that term in relation to them. A positive thing that autism professionals can do is to accept whatever autistic people tell them. So if someone wants to say they have special needs that's fine, and if they don't then that is also fine.

Learning difficulty. This can also be a tricky phrase. Yes autism may at times affect someone's ability to learn, but learn what? Does this mean learning in the sense of education, or social learning? Some autistic people will identify as having a 'learning difficulty', but there are many more who claim that autism does not affect their ability to learn. This term is no longer widely used, and the term 'learning disability' has taken its place, but it is still an acceptable term to some.

So what can you do as an autism professional?

It's hard to find a term that everyone with autism will be happy with, so often it's a case of working out what the individual likes, and sticking to this, rather than getting bogged down in definitions and dictionary terms. What you can do though is to listen to each person you work with, and let them guide you and help you in knowing how to refer to them. This will not only make them feel better around you, but will also help you to form a good working relationship with them.

#6

DON'T USE THE
WORD 'NORMAL'

You might find that you need to talk about people who do not have autism, and if you want to do so without saying the word 'normal', phrases like 'neuro-typical', or 'non-autistic' would be helpful. They are widely accepted in the autism community, and are often used by autistic people themselves.

Just think about what the word normal means. What does it mean to you, and also what might it mean to the person you are talking to? Normal might mean the standard set by other non-autistic people. A so-called normal person might not have a hard time using public transport, or might not find the change between weekday and weekend to be a big deal. Now to a degree that's fine; the majority of people are non-autistic, and therefore most likely don't have the same issues as autistic people have.

So this doesn't sound so bad, but if you think about it, by calling one part of society normal you indicate that the parts of society that don't match up to them are abnormal. You cannot use the word normal to describe someone without then – whether intentionally or not – attributing the word 'abnormal' to someone else. Most people would not think of this when using the term normal, but when you give it some thought, it seems clear that this will be the effect. When you look at it like this, it's easy for anyone to see why the term normal is frowned upon by the autistic community.

So going back to the first point, what do you say in place of the word normal? The phrase neuro-typical is often used, so is this a fully accepted way of talking about non-autistic people? Some say the term neuro-typical (or NT) is just another way of saying normal (and therefore it has the same negative implications), but most autistic people are more than happy with the use of this word. Using it may run the risk of offending some, but for the most part it is perfectly acceptable to say NT. The term NT does not split people into normal and abnormal groups, rather it characterises them as autistic or non-autistic. This might seem like a small thing to some, but to autistic people it can be huge; it means being autistic is not abnormal, it is just a different type of normal.

#7

....

THERE IS NOTHING 'MILD' ABOUT ASPERGER'S SYNDROME

One thing you could and should do as a professional is to think about each autistic person as an individual. Autism is a spectrum and you should think of it like this, rather than in terms of mild and severe – try to think about individual needs.

Asperger's syndrome is often talked about as being a mild form of autism, but this is not true at all. It is true that Asperger's might not be as visible as more classic autism, however, it is anything but mild. Lots of people with autism like to talk about the positive side of being autistic, and this is great, but they also readily face up to the challenges that can come with it. When someone with Asperger's hears it being downplayed as mild by someone who is meant to be helping them face these challenges, it can make things harder. The truth is that instead of having a 'mild' form of autism, people with Asperger's have the same traits and difficulties as those with classic autism, but they may present differently. In fact, the view that people with Asperger's have mild autism can often lead to people with Asperger's feeling under more pressure to fit into society. This can lead to them keeping up a front and living almost a double life, which can lead to anxiety, stress and depression. People with Asperger's will often be intelligent, and this can serve to mask the issues they might be having with their communication or social skills. But this does not mean the issues are not there, it just makes them harder to spot.

It's important for professionals to understand how people with autism feel about the term 'mild'. Most people with Asperger's say that they don't feel they are at one level, and in fact, they can struggle more or less with things depending on what kind of day they have had, how noisy the room is or just what time of day it is. Some days they might feel that their issues with independence or social skills, etc. are milder, but at other times they might feel they are huge, almost insurmountable issues. Understanding that one term cannot sum up the level of someone's issues is key here: Asperger's is best referred to simply as Asperger's, or even just autism. Some people would not bat an eyelid at being called mildly autistic, and some may even welcome it, but that's part of the issue. Saying mild autism is almost like saying 'you are autistic, but not that autistic', so it can be confusing to autistic people as well. The impact that autism in all its forms has on people on the spectrum and their families is far from mild. This is not to say that autism is wholly negative (this is not the case), but it does have an extreme impact on people's lives.

One thing you can do to help people is to talk to them about what impact they feel their autism is having on their life. This is much better than just assuming that as they have Asperger's the impact will not be that bad. It allows you to get to know them better, and also makes you better equipped to deal with any issues they do have. This approach would be more helpful to, and most likely better received by autistic people. It shows a greater understanding of autism, and how it does impact on peoples lives, rather than just trying to sum up that impact in one word. It also gives the professional a better insight into the autistic person and how they cope day to day, and even hour to hour, with some of the more negative aspects of autism.

#8

SAY 'ON THE SPECTRUM'

If you need to describe an autistic person and their autism, then referring to someone as 'on the spectrum' or 'on the autistic spectrum' is a nice, easy way of saying that someone is autistic without trying to sum up their level of need in one word. It is a term that is accepted by everyone, and one that is also understood by those who might not know a lot about autism. It's true that it does not go into great detail about the individual, but this is better than using a term that looks on the surface as if it is detailed, but in reality is flawed, for example, 'mild autism'.

Given that it is factual, accurate and not likely to offend anyone, it's a nice simple way of saying that someone is autistic without running the risk of offending by using incorrect terminology, or downplaying any part of their autism. There are no fixed points on the spectrum, so describing someone as being 'on the spectrum' allows you to remain flexible when talking about their autism, and how it affects them.

#9

....

ADDRESS THE PERSON DIRECTLY

People with autism – the same as anyone else – like to be spoken to, rather than about. A small disclaimer here is that a lot of people with autism will ask for questions to be addressed to a family member, and that's fine. If you do end up talking to the parent or care giver, then you could still try and include the autistic person in a positive way by referring back to them. For example, you might say 'Does that sound good to you?' Or check with them that they are happy with the way the conversation is going. Don't just let it happen around them, and pass them by. But as a professional it's best to wait and see if this is what they would like, rather than just assuming. So while it is true that many autistic people will not want to talk, or be addressed directly, many will, and find not being addressed directly to be disrespectful. There is nothing wrong with asking someone straight out if they want you to address them or someone else at the start of your meeting. It won't seem like an odd question to anyone who knows anything about autism.

Not addressing someone directly when they want you to can appear very disrespectful and rude. There have been times when autistic adults who have taken a parent or sibling into a meeting for support have had a professional come in and say hello to that sibling/parent, and go on to say 'Does such and such mind if I shake his hand?' It's clear to see why the autistic person would be offended by this – it takes them out of the meeting, and reduces them to the role of a passive spectator, while the professional, and whomever they are talking to, discuss them. So make sure you address the person directly, unless requested not to.

#10

REFER TO PARENTS BY NAME

When speaking to the parents of an autistic individual refer to them by name. Referring to parents by their name does not mean saying to the autistic child or adult 'So is this Bob?' instead of 'So is this your dad?' What it does mean is trying not to say things like 'So what do you think about this, Mum?' when referring to the autistic person's mother. Maybe there is nothing wrong with this, but some autistic people do have an issue with it. First of all, it sounds a bit odd calling someone who is not *your* mum or dad, Mum or Dad. And second, it is quite a childish way to talk around someone, and often professionals can be in such a habit of doing this that they will talk this way to the parents of teenagers, and even adults. It is much better just to use names, e.g. 'What do you think, Mrs Moran?' This is a more respectful and grown-up way to talk rather than saying 'What does Mum think?' Now this might not be the case when dealing with a very young child, or even some older individuals, if they indicate that they prefer it, but overall it is best. It sounds more respectful, not only to the adult you are addressing, but also to the person with autism, who may well be an adult themselves. It is extremely inportant at this point to stress that this is not a huge issue, and you don't need to worry if this is something you are in the habit of doing, but it is something that might be worth thinking about. It might be that what you should do is look at each situation on its own merits, and make sure you take the age of the autistic person into account.

#11

ADAPTING YOUR
LANGUAGE AND THE
WAY YOU SPEAK

Building on the point about neutral language, you can adapt your language depending on whom you are talking to in order to make them feel more comfortable, and to help in obtaining better channels of communication with them.

Everyone with autism is different, and this means that language has to be adapted to suit whomever it is you happen to be talking to at the time. There is no point in having a set way of talking that you try and apply to all autistic people as, though it might be perfect for some, it might not work at all for others. You might have to adapt your language and the way you speak due to age, level of understanding or simply due to how stressed and overloaded someone might be on any given day. Some people with autism might be more able to understand what is being said to them so you would be able to use unsimplified language, whereas others might have a hard time understanding what is being said, and you might have to simplify, or even use a visual way of communicating with them. Using visual cues and simple language is great, but you will need to adapt this if it is clear that someone is understanding what is being said without the need for it. There is no point just sticking with it, as it's what you're used to – this can come across as being highly patronising. If you have the ability to tell that someone is understanding what is being said, you can change your language and perhaps ask them if they feel they need the visual aid. By the same token, you might be talking to someone who normally understands very well, but they might have had a long and overwhelming bus ride before the meeting, and feel overloaded. So what you are saying will likely not be making any sense to them if this is the case, and therefore there is nothing to be gained by continuing in the same way as usual. This would be a vital time to adapt the way you are talking to ensure that the autistic individual gets the benefit of what you are saying to them. You might slow down your speech, and explain in a very basic way, trying to cut out unnecessary detail and deviations from the subject. Being able to adapt the way you speak, and not just having one way of talking that you try and apply to all people, at all times, will be a huge help to you and the autistic individuals with whom you are working.

#12

YOU WILL BE TAKEN LITERALLY

Say what you mean without using 'sayings', and referring to things that could be misunderstood by people with autism. This will make things much clearer, and avoid misunderstandings.

Working with autistic people can throw up a lot of surprises and be pretty unpredictable, but one thing you can be sure of is that if you are working with autistic people you will be taken literally – a lot. This is just one of the things about having autism; some people will do it often, and some hardly ever, but it would be a very rare autistic person who never took anything literally. You might think that this means you have to watch what you say at all times, and in a way it does, but this does not have to be a stressful and hard-to-manage process. Everyone has habits when it comes to the way they talk: certain things they say often, stock responses and a way of ordering their words. All you need to do is make sure you form the right habits, and then after a while you will talk the right way without even having to think about it. Think about things such as sayings and idioms – however common they are, they might end up being taken the wrong way. There have been cases where people with autism were scared to go in to work as they overheard someone they worked with saying that they would 'kill' another employee. Now, most people will say something like 'I'll kill him!' at some point, and mean nothing by it. It's a throw-away phrase, and sometimes it is not even said with any anger at all behind it. But if someone with autism takes it literally, it's easy to see why it would unsettle them. Again, it's about professionals being able to get into the mindset of the people with whom they are working. But however hard most people try, they will still be taken literally at times – even autistic people say things that get taken literally, and are misunderstood by other autistic people – so the aim is to cut down on this, and not to worry if it still happens from time to time. It is important to point out that some autistic people do understand common sayings and idioms, but this links back the point about being able to adjust your language depending on who you are talking to. And it might be worth just sticking to not using them to help you form good habits.

#13

....

SARCASM

One of the best and most positive things you can do when talking to autistic people is to avoid using sarcasm. Going back to the point about being taken literally, sarcasm is often taken this way and is therefore not always understood by people with autism. Avoiding it would be a positive way of helping autistic people to feel better about talking to you.

Sarcasm is something a lot of autistic people just don't get, but it goes beyond this: it is quite common to hear people with autism say that sarcasm is cruel and pointless. Now it is true that there is nothing wrong with being a bit sarcastic every now and then, but due to the lack of understanding, and sometimes hatred, that autistic people can have when it comes to sarcasm, it is best to avoid it. What you have to do is think about how sarcasm works: you say something sarcastic, and the only thing that makes it a joke rather than an insult is the tone of voice you use. Well, if someone is unable to differentiate between tones of voice, how are they meant to know you are not insulting them? Or if they ask a question, and you say 'yes' in a sarcastic way, how are they meant to know that you actually mean 'no' if they cannot understand your tone of voice? If you use sarcasm and someone does not understand it, then you might think you are coming across as funny, and easy to get on with, but instead the autistic individual might just view you as rude, and even a bit silly.

Luckily this is an easy thing to fix – all you need to do is think before you speak, and don't be sarcastic. Sarcasm is a form of humour, so it can be cut out of the way you speak without having to affect anything you are saying. It's not key to the way you talk, and in fact it's something a lot of people try and do knowingly. Like a lot of the tips in this book it comes down to habit: if you are in the habit of being sarcastic when you talk – as a lot of people are – then you might have to think about the way you speak in your day-to-day life even when not dealing with autistic people. If you change this, and cut down on your use of sarcasm, you will form new habits that will help you in your work with autistic people. Not using sarcasm will not only make it easier for people with autism to understand you, but it might make them like you a bit more!

Some autistic people will understand and even use sarcasm, but on the whole it is not something you should be using when talking to them. It can be hard for some autistic people who use sarcasm, as people don't expect them to, and therefore don't pick up on it! So it goes both ways…

#14

THE USE OF FUNCTIONING LABELS

You can talk about people as having autism without saying that they are 'high functioning' or 'low functioning'. Functioning labels are a controversial topic. They are used a lot, and the people who do use them claim that they are necessary to detail the level of need someone with autism might have. But those who dislike them say that, far from being helpful, they are in fact misleading, and do not give any detail on an individual's level of need. Autism is complex, and it presents differently in different people. People with autism themselves say that the terms high and low functioning do not represent them, as they will have different levels of need from day to day. Also, they might be unable to do one thing, but be fine doing another – functioning labels do not allow for this level of detail. Now this is where it gets a bit complicated: functioning labels are the norm, and as a professional it might be expected of you to use them, but autistic people don't like them, so what do you do?

If someone makes it clear they do not like the terms high or low functioning, then it is not fair to use them. It might be commonplace to use these terms where you work, but a more positive thing would be to respect the wishes of whomever you are working with, and just write down that they are on the spectrum. Some people who are classed as high functioning like the term, as it implies that they are smarter than other autistic people, but as a professional you don't need to feel that you have to play into that. The term high functioning can, in fact, lead to an autistic person being denied services, and mask the level to which they are struggling. And it is okay for you to point this out to them.

However, you should be aware that if you do record something in this way, i.e. high or low functioning, it will be there for years to come. Other professionals, years down the line, might read it, and it could end up affecting their work with the individual. But more than this, try and think about what these labels mean when you say them – if you say someone is low functioning, what does that mean? Are you saying that they can't do anything? Are you saying they have a harder time doing things than most? Or are you saying that they struggle with some things? The truth is you might be trying to say one thing, and neuro-typical people hearing it might think something else, while autistic people hearing it might think something completely different. It's all a matter of perception, and functioning labels do not mean the same thing to everyone. There is a need for detail when talking about the level of ability and need someone with autism has, and functioning labels just do not give that level of detail. One of the best things you can do is to observe the autistic person – not just once, but on different days – see how they cope with things after a quiet day, and then again after a long, busy day. Take into account as much as you can, and see as much as you can – don't just think that as they were able, or unable to do something one day, you can put a label on them. Autistic people will be more able to function on some days than others; one day they might be able to do a lot, but they might then crash and be unable to do anything for the next two days.

The term high functioning can in fact mask how much someone is struggling. It can hinder them getting the help they need, and also make them feel as if they should not be struggling as much as they are. A term like low functioning is just plain offensive, and it should be easy to see why. People's IQs should not been viewed as a mark of how much they struggle with their autism; often people with higher IQs are classed as high functioning. But while they might have above average intelligence, that does not mean they don't struggle as much as any other autistic person within social situations, for example.

It's best just to say someone is on the spectrum, or is autistic, without trying to place them on a scale of 'autisticness'. As stated above, a person's autism may present differently from day to day, and can often change, and affect them differently from one hour to the next. No overall label is a substitute for observing this, and taking the time to understand it.

#15

NON-VERBAL VS PRE-VERBAL

The term 'non-verbal' has been widely used to describe someone who either does not talk at all, or hardly talks; for example, someone who only says one or two words, or speaks very rarely. But there seems to be a trend among parents and professionals to replace this with the term 'pre-verbal'. This implies that the individual will become verbal one day. While this might be the case sometimes, often people will in fact remain non-verbal for the whole of their lives.

The issue with this is that a lot of autistic people who identify as non-verbal dislike the term pre-verbal. They feel that it has a kind of 'never giving up hope' feel to it. It makes them feel as if people see them as somehow lacking because they do not talk – the implication being that they are stuck in a stage of their development that they will one day pass out of. In fact, the autistic individual might see not talking as just a part of who they are, and as something they are happy to live with for the rest of their life. There are some people who are non-verbal, and wish to talk but can't. But there are others who are happy the way they are, and make themselves understood and communicate without speech. Non-verbal people can, and often do, live the same kinds of lives as anyone else.

It is important for professionals to make sure they treat all forms of communication with the same level of respect. Therefore, if someone feels they are not pre-verbal as they don't ever want to be verbal, or know they never will be and are happy with this, then that should be respected. The point here really is just to be sure to respect whatever the autistic person wants. It might well be that some autistic people like to think of themselves as being pre-verbal, and in that case it's fine to refer to them as such, but for the most part, autistic people prefer the phrase non-verbal. Pre-verbal seems to be one of those phrases that is used mostly by parents who seem to be living in hope of their children talking one day. But when it comes to professionals, the language that should be used is that which is favoured by autistic people themselves, and not by their families or by other professionals.

It can be hard for some non-verbal autistic people to make clear which phrase they prefer. It might be that they can type, or use some other means of making their voices heard. However, they might never be able to make it clear what they do want. All that can be done in this case is to go by the views given by non-verbal people who are able to express what they feel. And this seems to be to use the term non-verbal, and not pre-verbal.

#16

....

PRE-CONCEIVED IDEAS

You should go into meetings with autistic people with an open mind, setting aside all pre-conceived ideas about them, and about autism as a whole.

One of the most harmful things to autistic people is pre-conceived ideas about autism. These can come from media stereotypes, functioning labels or even dealings someone has had in the past with other autistic people. It has been said before, but it's worth saying again – all autistic people are different. There is no one thing that is true for every autistic person, and therefore there is no point sitting down with pre-conceived ideas about them as people. You have to take the time to get to know whomever you are talking to, and should not think that it is as easy as finding out how autistic people work; chat to them as much as you can, and find out who they are, and what they like. Try to discover what they find hard, and what they are confident about, and get to know them as people as best you can. Chatting will not work for everyone and that's fine, you can do drawings or other visual activities to find out about them. If you have to you can get the information from someone who knows them well, and build up to being able to interact with them in this way.

It is quite easy to tell when someone has sat down with a set of preconceived ideas in their head, and it makes the whole process of talking a lot harder for the autistic person. Not only do they have to speak – which they might find hard – but they also have to break through this set of ideas before they can even move on to the process of getting the help they need. But it's not just hard for them; you as a professional will find it hard to get anywhere if your ideas are wrong from the start. You have to go into each meeting with the understanding that you are talking to an individual, and not just someone who fits into a set of ideas you might have formed over the years. By doing this you will ensure a more relaxed meeting, and also a more open and friendly relationship with whomever you are working with.

#17

....

APPEARANCES CAN
BE DECEPTIVE

Not making judgements about people based on how they look is a positive quality in anyone and being able to carry this into your professional life is one of the most positive things you can do.

There are a lot of cliches that can be used to make this point, e.g. 'don't judge a book by its cover', but there is some truth to sayings like this. On the surface someone might appear fully confident and relaxed – they might be chatting away, and look as if they are dealing with the situation well (the situation could be a meeting or an assessment), but part of being a good professional, and working with people with autism, is being able to look past the surface, and trying to work out what is going on inside. People with autism tend not to show too much on the outside, and this is why so much of their 'behaviour' can appear to be unpredictable and random.

But things such as meltdowns and overloads have build ups – sometimes very long build ups. The trick to being able to detect them is to see what is going on under the surface. But, how do we do that?

Well, one of the most obvious ways is just to try and talk to the autistic individual; they might not be able to say what they are feeling, but they might indicate that they feel a bit strange, or are starting to feel a bit overwhelmed. Sometimes people with autism don't volunteer information, but when asked will be happy to disclose it. It won't work every time, but it's a good, basic way of finding out what someone is thinking or feeling – just ask them. You might also ask by getting them to indicate a visual aid that shows how they are feeling – happy or sad faces maybe. You could also give them a sign that they can hold up to show how they are feeling; for example, a sign that says 'You are talking too loudly', or a sign that shows an image of someone with their hands over their ears. Having something they can hold up might just be easier for someone with autism than having to speak up, and say how they are feeling. Some autistic people are also non-verbal and this is a good way of helping them communicate. There might also be a bit of trial and error – it could be that you can't tell what is going on under the surface to start with, but after a while you should develop a relationship with whomever you are working with, and part of that is getting to know what certain things about them mean. If the autistic individual seems to be finding it hard to understand things you are saying, when at the start of your meeting they were doing fine, you might know that this means they are starting to experience a sensory overload.

It also goes the other way: someone might not be verbal, and on the surface might not look as if they understand what is going on. They might not be looking at you, and might not be responding much when you talk, but that is not the whole picture. Inside they might be well aware of what is going on, and might even want to look at you, or respond but are unable to do so. Many autistic people can concentrate and understand things better if they are not looking at the person who is speaking. It means they do not get overloaded and can think just about what is being said without being overwhelmed by needless sensory details. This can make them look uninterested or rude, but that is not the case, it is just a coping mechanism. Some non-verbal, autistic people have a hard time being taken seriously even though they can articulate their thoughts and understanding as well as anyone else through typing or writing.

The point is that what you see on the surface is just that; there is more behind it for everyone, and especially for people with autism, who often find it hard to express emotions on the outside. Someone might not be verbal, they might be chatting away, they might have a blank face or they might be constantly smiling, but whatever they are doing on the outside does not mean that it matches what is going on inside. There is another cliche 'it's what's on the inside that counts' – again there is truth to this – to truly understand someone, and what is going on for them, you have to know what is in their mind, not just what shows on their face.

#18

TRIAD OF IMPAIRMENTS

One thing you can do as a professional is to think about more positive, or at least more neutral, ways to explain the triad. For example, instead of saying someone has an inpairment in their social skills, you could just say that people with autism often find social situations hard.

The term 'Triad of Impairments' is one that is used a lot. It is made up of communication, interaction and imagination. It is used so much that it might be hard to see why anyone would have an issue with it, but all you have to do is think about the wording – impairments. It's not really a nice word to hear in reference to yourself, is it? A lot of non-autistic people are unimaginative, but they would not be called imagination-impaired. To say someone has difficulty communicating, or has some issues with their communication sounds a lot better than saying they are in some way impaired. It's to do with thinking about the way you phrase things; you need to bear in mind that the things you say apply to real-life people who will have to carry the things that are said, or written about them around for life. So the difference between saying 'has some trouble communicating' and 'is communication-impaired' can be huge. What you say as a professional can impact on the autistic individual's self-esteem and self-belief. If they are made to feel that they are impaired as an individual, then how are they meant to accept that their autism is an important part of them, and does not mean they are somehow inferior to other, non-autistic people? Words have power, and you have to remember this when dealing with autistic people.

The term Triad of Impairments itself is flawed: a lot of autistic people have vivid and very active imaginations, so to imply that a lack of imagination is a key sign of autism just plays into the stereotype. Yes, there can be a lack of what is known as social imagination, but again the phrasing is wrong, so how are we to know if this is meant or not? Autistic people can have rigid thought processes, and sometimes this can make it look as if they have issues with their imagination, when they do not. Now it is true that issues with interactions and communication are a big part of most people's autism, but they are just that – issues. Talking about them in a less negative way will help you get better responses out of the autistic people you are working with.

#19

....

GIFTEDNESS IS
NOT A GIVEN

One common misconception about people with autism is that they will have some special skill or, failing that, at least a high level of intellect. This is just not true. It would be nice to think that everyone with autism is amazing at maths or able to learn any musical instrument, but the truth is, autistic people have the same skills as anyone else. Some people are great at stuff, some are not, but it is important that when talking to autistic people professionals do not assume they will have some special skill or giftedness.

Assuming that someone will have a high intellect because they have Asperger's syndrome or so-called 'high functioning' autism is not the way to go. While it is true that Asperger's often goes hand-in-hand with high levels of intelligence, this should not be assumed when coming into contact with people who have Asperger's.

But perhaps the most simple, and yet important thing to avoid doing is asking someone 'What is your special skill?' This is something autistic people often get asked, and most people with autism find it very trying. Some autistic people might have all kinds of skills – some might be related to their autism and some might not. But not all autistic people have a Rain Man-type skill. The thing is, a lot, if not most professionals know this, and would never ask that question. But for the few out there who would, it might be better just to ask about the autistic person in a different way. It's okay to ask them what they do for fun, and to ask the same questions that might be asked of anyone else, autistic or not.

Also be sure not to get special interests mixed up with skills. Someone might have a special interest in cars and count the cars that go by, talk about cars all day and basically appear to think and talk about cars more than anything else. But that does not mean they will have some car-based skill. They might not be able to drive, and they might have no clue how the inside of a car works. Autistic people are just like anyone else, and they can take an interest in something without having to be skilled in that field. It is fine to talk to someone with autism about their special interest, but it is not good to assume that because they like it they will be skilled it in. The best thing to do is just to talk to them about it in the same way that you would with anyone else who was talking about a hobby.

Autistic people might be what is thought of as gifted, smart or skilled at something, but so could anyone else be. Autism itself does not mean someone is going to be smart or skilful. The best, and most positive way of dealing with autistic people is to treat them like anyone else as much as possible. Of course this doesn't mean not doing things to help them feel more comfortable, but it does mean avoiding making assumptions about them.

#20

....

AUTISM IS
A NEUROLOGICAL
CONDITION

One of the best things you can do to make a positive impression right from the start is to get your terminology right. Saying that autism is a 'neurological condition' rather than a mental illness shows that you know what you are talking about.

Now this is a big issue, and one of the biggest challenges that autistic people face with professionals of any kind: autism is not a mental health issue, it is a neurological issue. Rather than being a mental health issue that has developed over time, autism is something people are born with. The brain does not change and become autistic; autistic people are born with brains that work differently from those around them – and this is not the same as having a mental health issue. Now there is nothing wrong with having a mental health issue – and professionals should not think that autistic people think there is – but you have to get stuff right; how can you as a professional be expected to be taken seriously if you use the wrong terminology all the time? The key issue here is making sure that you use the correct terminology, or you will fail to inspire confidence in the people you are working with. Treating autism as a mental health condition makes it sound as if you do not even understand the very basic concept of autism - if that's your starting point, then however good you are, it will be hard to recover from.

This will undermine anything you go on to say, as the people you are talking to may not believe that you are competent. This is not to say that you are not, but it's about how you present yourself. The autistic brain is 'wired differently', and this is not the same as having a mental health condition. If you get this right, then you will start off sounding a lot more competent.

There is a wider issue here about what kind of training people get regarding autism, and how this should be specialised, and not just lumped in with mental health training. The thing to take from this is that autistic people – more often than not – know and understand their condition, and the terminology relating to it. And if they don't, their family will. If you show that you know and understand this, you will get on a lot better with the people you are working with, and this will make your job that much easier to do.

Autistic people can often have mental health issues such as depression and anxiety alongside their autism. The autism can be the root cause of these issues, often due to the autistic person finding it so hard to fit into and deal with the world around them, but you must not get this mixed up, and think that they are one and the same. However, it is true that to tackle the mental health issue, sometimes you do have to look at issues that might be affected by the individual's autism.

#21

....

AUTISTIC PERSON, NOT PATIENT

As with the point about mental health conditions, showing that you have a good understanding of autism from the start can be a positive step in forming a good working relationship with someone who has autism. So by avoiding inaccurate medical terms when talking about autism you show respect to autistic people, as well as showing them that you understand autism. Just as autism is not a mental health issue, neither is it a medical one. It is not a disease, and it does not have 'sufferers' – the autistic individual you are working with is not a patient. As previously mentioned, autism is a different 'wiring of the brain', and not something that is medically treatable. It's true that people with autism will need help at times, but this is not medical help related to their autism. The ways that work best for dealing with the issues that autism throws up are not medical treatments – they are based on talking, planning, routine and trying to understand feelings. One of the main issues people with autism have to deal with is being told that there is an 'epidemic' of autism, or that the number of autism 'sufferers' has gone up. When you use medical terms such as 'autistic patients' you play into this culture of medicalising autism, and treating autism as though it is a disease.

You are working with people to help them, that is true, but this does not make them your patients. What you do call them is a bit harder, but do you really need to call them anything? They are people you work with, when you talk about them you will be using their names anyway. But it's throw-away bits of conversation where this tends to be more of an issue. Things like 'Don't worry, I can help with that. I had another patient last year with the same thing.' This, and things like it, are not said with any intention of harm, but nevertheless they can, and often do, cause offence. Like most of the points in this book, it can be dealt with by just thinking a bit before you speak – instead of saying you had a patient just say you worked with someone last year who had the same issue. It's a small thing, but to people with autism it can be a very big deal as it connects to a massive issue in the autism community – the misinformed idea that autism is a disease or epidemic.

#22

NO NEED TO GRIEVE

One thing you can do from the very start is to remain positive, or at least neutral, when diagnosing someone with autism. One huge part of that is not telling the parents of said newly diagnosed autistic individual that they need to 'grieve for the child they should have had'. By avoiding using this 'saying', you can, in fact, have a hugely positive impact on how the family views the autistic person. Let's make one thing clear: I understand, as someone with autism, that it might take the family a while to adjust. They might be scared for what their child's life will be like, that they might become a victim of bullying or hate crime. So they will need a bit of time to get used to this, to think it through and to understand what it all means, and grow to accept it. Parents also need this time to learn about autism, and to understand that a diagnosis of autism does not mean their child will never make anything of their lives. They might go on to do great things, or they may do smaller things that are great to them. Fine, but that is not grieving. Grieving is what you do if someone dies, so is that meant to imply that autism is akin to a death sentence? No it's not. That's not why professionals say it, but whether that's what is meant or not, that's still what it sounds like. Of course parents need time to think and adjust, it's just that saying someone should 'take the time to grieve for the child they should have had' is not only insulting, but also sends out a very odd message. It's not as if autistic people come in place of someone else – there never was another child that should have been born, and therefore there is no one to grieve for. I understand the point of it: what it is saying is take all the things you thought your child would be like, and put them to one side. Get used to the fact that your child might never talk – they might, but they might not. Put aside your daydreams, and take a few days to do that in your own time. And saying that might be a positive message for professionals to give. It takes away the concept of grief. I can understand that people need time to get used to the fact that what they had in their head is not matching up to real life, that's fine, but as a professional, a positive and forward-thinking thing you could do is to broach this without bringing up the idea of grieving. By not bringing grief into it, you can make diagnosis a more positive time for families. Yes your child is autistic and things will be different, but this is your child – there is no other child you should have had, this is the child you were meant to have.

#23

....

PUZZLING

The idea that autistic people are puzzles that need to be solved by neuro-typical people has been around for years. It is represented by the image of the puzzle piece, which in some illustrations can even be seen to be missing from someone's head, as if part of the brain is missing. Some autistic people have no issues with this, but there are those in the autism community who dislike the idea that autistic people are a puzzle to be solved. And the language used by professionals can have a huge impact on this.

The image itself is one thing, but this book is dealing with language, and the use of the words 'puzzling' or 'puzzle' should be avoided. If a professional is talking either to someone, or worse, about them, in front of them, and that autistic person hears themselves and their behaviour being described as a puzzle, a few things can happen. First, it does not fill them full of confidence that said professional will be of help to them. Second, and more importantly, it cuts them off. It creates a feeling of difference and separation.

The professional is not working with them to help them through whatever they are having trouble with, they are instead studying them, and trying to decode them.

No one likes to be thought of as being a mystery. One of the best things professionals can do is to talk to the autistic person, and explain how they feel in different, more positive ways. There is nothing wrong with them saying they do not know why someone is doing or feeling something. But it should not be said in such a way that the autistic person feels it is their fault. Saying 'I don't understand' is different from saying 'You are a puzzle'. Autistic people want to feel that they are being treated the same as everyone else, and are not seen as somehow alien or different.

Professionals who do not treat or talk about autistic people as if they are a puzzle to be decoded will often have much more positive and helpful interactions with them.

#24

....

FACIAL EXPRESSIONS

Facial expressions can be tricky things for people with autism. Sometimes autistic people can completely misread facial expressions – well, to tell the truth, they are misread more often than not. That is why a lot of work is done to help autistic people understand facial expressions. Often this is done using visual aids, but even with this it is worth thinking about how much you might be using them to express yourself to someone who is just not understanding. This is not to say that you need to keep your face blank, but try and say what you are thinking instead of indicating it with your face, and expecting the autistic individual to pick up on it. People express a lot with their face, and that's fine, but do it along with talking, not instead of, and you should be okay.

Someone with autism might be able to follow part of what you are saying, but if you are only trying to convey something using your face, there is very little chance that they will pick up on it. People with autism might not even notice that your expression has changed. So it may not even be a case of them misunderstanding your expression, your face might just look blank to them. A lot of autistic individuals don't even look at people's faces when they are talking, and even if we are looking, we might miss a face changing from happy to sad. It sounds odd, but autistic people tend to be a lot better at seeing the small details, and can often miss the bigger, more obvious things. The best way to let us autistic people know how you are feeling is just to tell us. Doing work to help us understand and read facial expressions is great, but you can't rely on it straight away. The best communication is based on saying what you need the other person to know, or using a visual aid if necessary. If you do wish to communicate something, then just say it, and don't hint at it in ways the autistic person might not understand.

#25

....

BODY LANGUAGE

Like facial expressions, body language is a language that most autistic people just do not understand. It is a huge part of how people communicate, and it would be pointless to say it's not – that's where a lot of autistic people's communication issues come from. Not being able to understand a huge part of how others communicate is not easy. You cannot always do something about your body language, but what you can do is to understand that however much you might think something is clear from your body language, unless you say it, there is no guarantee that someone with autism will be able to pick up on it.

If someone is talking too much, and you want to get away, you might take half a step back, or glance down at your watch. This is a hint that you need to be going. It's not rude, or even an overly obvious signal, but you expect whomever you are talking to to pick up on it and let you get going. But you might well find that someone with autism will not even notice. Most people know that autistic people find reading body language hard, but it's funny how many times they don't think about this when talking to autistic people.

You don't need to think you are being rude if you just come right out and tell someone with autism what you wish they would pick up on. In fact, you're being far from rude, you're talking to them in a way that they understand, instead of trying to give them hints in a language they just don't understand. You don't have to think about keeping your own body language in check, but just make sure you don't start to rely on it to communicate in the same way you might do when talking to someone who is not autistic. The thing to think about here is that you are trying to communicate with someone, and there is no point trying this if you are going to use a form of language they do not understand. So, for your benefit as much as theirs, you should try and make sure you say everything out loud, or communicate using visual aids if necessary, to be sure that they understand what it is you are communicating to them.

#26

....

ENVIRONMENT

If you are having a meeting, assessment or even an informal chat with someone who has autism, then you need to spend a bit of time beforehand thinking about the environment. Is it too bright? Is it too noisy? How many people are going to be there? What can be seen out of the windows? Has it got air conditioning? Noisy pipes? Or, to put it a bit more simply, try and think of somewhere nice and quiet, not too bright or busy and do the meeting, assessment or chat there. People with autism have a strong eye and ear for detail, and although that can be great, it also means it's very easy for us to become overwhelmed. If you want to meet in your office, try and ensure that there will not be people making a lot of noise outside the door the whole time. If you want to chat, then maybe don't pick a very busy café in the middle of the day. It's something that you might not think of right away, and that's fine, but once you get into the habit of thinking about where you are going to talk, it becomes a lot easier. You don't really have to ask yourself 20 questions before each meeting, all you have to do is bear in mind how the environment might affect the autistic person. Is it going to be so busy and loud they won't be able to think and answer you, or is it going to be nice and relaxed for them so that they can think clearly? Of course letting the autistic person pick where you meet is a good option, but even then you do have to have a think about it, and if you feel it might be overwhelming, it's okay to speak up and say so.

An overwhelming environment can lead to a total overload and shutdown in someone with autism, and one thing you do need to think about is that if someone with autism expresses any feelings of discomfort in the environment you have picked, it might be worth changing it. When we become overloaded, it becomes harder for us to understand things that are being said, and to think clearly, so not only does that make things quite unpleasant for us, it also makes your job a lot harder!

#27

....

PHYSICAL CONTACT

Making physical contact is something that autistic people can find hard, and even a light touch might feel uncomfortable, or even painful. This is why they might react in a negative, and seemingly over-the-top way to something you think is a small and natural thing to do. It might appear to be rude if someone with autism does not shake your hand if you offer it, or pulls away if you try and put your hand on their shoulder, but it is not – what you have to bear in mind is that in most circumstances when someone autistic is meeting with a professional, it will be overwhelming and difficult for them anyway, so that extra level of discomfort with the physical contact is something they will avoid if they can. This is not to say you can't make any physical contact with someone who is autistic: you could ask if it's okay to shake hands or not when you first meet them, and then make it a habit to ask before you make contact. If someone says no, then you need to respect this.

It's hard to explain why physical contact can be so hard, as how it feels varies from person to person. To some it might feel painful, as if even a light touch is akin to someone grabbing them and digging their fingers into their skin. To others it might not hurt, but will feel like a discomfort – this might be mild, or it might be so bad that they have to pull away. Now this is not just a physical feeling, it's how the mind reacts, so any one individual might react in a different way each time. To the autistic individual, someone's hand might feel too hot, too cold, too dry or just about anything else.

There is also the issue of overload to consider: some people are fine with physical contact most of the time, but when they are having a sensory overload they feel overwhelmed and hemmed in as it is. They start to feel claustrophobic, and someone touching them just adds to this in the worst way. If someone is having an overload or a meltdown, then try not to touch them – it might be tempting to, and yes, at times, if they are hurting themselves or someone else, you might have to, but avoid doing so whenever possible. As long as no one is at risk, try and help them to relax without touching them or talking too much. A good rule to stick to is to simply try and avoid any and all unnecessary physical contact with autistic people as by and large, they will not like it.

#28

....

HAVE A TIME LIMIT
ON THE SESSION

Having a time limit on meetings and assessments is one of the most important things you can do as a professional working with autistic people. We need routine and plans, and knowing when something starts and finishes can be helpful to us. It also means that we are less likely to become overloaded, and therefore get more from the session. But sticking to the time limit is the important part: it's easy to say that a meeting will last an hour, but it seems to be harder to stick to this. The thing is, this can throw people with autism, and sometimes that change can take us weeks to fully get out of our system. If someone is being assessed, and they have been told it will last an hour, yet two hours later they are still there, that would be stressful for anyone, but for someone who needs structure and routine and a clear plan, it can be extremely hard.

The best thing to do is to work out what it is you plan to do with the autistic person beforehand, and then plan how long you think that will take, maybe overestimating the time just in case there are any delays. That way you can let them know well in advance what is planned, and write it down as well. A visual timetable can be helpful for the autistic person. Make sure you stick to the plan no matter how things seem on the day. The autistic person might seem happy to go off-plan, and stay for longer, but try and avoid asking them to do so – they might not feel the impact of the change of plan immediately, but that does not mean it will not have an impact. It might not fully hit them until a few days later, and it might result in sensory overload, meltdowns or shutdowns.

The best thing you can do when you have made a plan with someone who is autistic is to stick to it, but sometimes even the autistic person will need reminding of that. They might indicate to you that they want to change the plans at short notice; for example, they might request that the meeting be longer than planned. Depending on why they were asking, you might feel you need to say yes, but most of the time it would be best not to change the plan. If you explain to them why you feel that way, they should understand. It can be easy, even for autistic people themselves, to underestimate quite how big and far-reaching the impact of changes to routine/plans can be. Changes can't always be helped, but when they can be avoided they should be.

#29

OFFER BREAKS DURING SESSIONS

Sessions and meetings can be overwhelming for people with autism, and the longer they drag on, the less able autistic people are to focus on what is being said, and join in. Often they will need a break so that they are able to come back and avoid a full-on overload where they cannot really take in or understand what is being said to them. However, it is true that autistic people can find it hard to ask for a break, even more so if they are close to being overloaded, so it falls to the professional to offer the break when they feel it is needed, or to help the autistic person to be able to ask for a break. This might be done through the use of a sign, to be shown by the autistic person when they are in need of a break.

It might be best to pre-plan when the breaks are going to be. When someone with autism is starting to get overloaded, sometimes they find it hard to make decisions, and they might not be able to think clearly. Therefore, when asked if they want a break, they might say no, even if they actually do want one. Also, it is much better to stop someone getting to the point when they need a rest than to get them to that point, and only then offer a rest.

Pre-planning rests is a good way to get the most out of a session. There is no point working with someone with autism after they become too overloaded. An overload can rob someone of their ability to think clearly, and to understand what is being said. It can stop autistic people from being able to communicate, and lead to them being unable to follow what is going on. It is worth taking breaks to avoid getting to this point.

It might be that a sign is used so that even if the autistic person does not feel able to talk, they can still show this to indicate they want a break. This would have to be agreed upon and talked about beforehand, and there might still be an issue with them not knowing when they need to break until it is too late.

So pre-planned breaks are best, but breaks might still need to be offered. If a professional can see that someone with autism is becoming overwhelmed, they might need to offer a break instead of waiting for the autistic person to ask for one. Also, the phrasing is important. Perhaps saying something like 'I want us to take a short break, will that be okay with you?' instead of 'Do you want to take a short break?' might be best. In some cases, if the autistic person has not been thinking of taking a break they might say no, but if the professional can see a break is needed, it is okay to call for one.

Often, if autistic people are asked something they have not had time to think about they will just say yes or no without really knowing what they are saying – this is due to difficulty in making decisions, especially when they are feeling overwhelmed. Then, as time goes on, and they can think clearly, they might regret this. Keep this in mind when it comes to offering breaks. Sometimes it is better just to say 'It's time for a break' than to ask. Someone with autism could easily just say no, as they were not expecting the question.

#30

. . . .

EXPLAIN WHAT WILL
BE HAPPENING,
AND WHEN

In the same way that making a clear plan for the time of the session will be helpful, you should also plan what you will be doing, and when, in the session. This helps autistic people, as they have a plan for what is going to happen, and things are not being sprung on them. This will help them to relax, and to get the most out of their meeting with you. It would be best if you gave them this information some time before you meet up, but, failing that, the next best thing to do is to sit down with them before you start, and talk them through what it is you will be doing, and in what order you will be doing it. Again, the point of doing this is to help them relax, so if you do make a plan you need to try your best to stick to it no matter what. This level of planning might seem over the top, but if you tell someone what you are doing and not in what order, then that does not really make things any better, but if you tell them both, you will alleviate a lot of their stress. The one thing you do need to watch out for though is that you don't overwhelm the autistic person. You do need to explain things, but try to do it as briefly as you can. Get all your information into a few key sentences and then leave it at that, or you might overwhelm the autistic person and bring on an overload. You might also think about doing a visual chart to help them; writing down everything that is going to happen, when it will happen and how long you think it will take. People with autism often find things easier to follow if they can see them instead of just going on what someone is saying, so it would be worth taking the time to write this out just so that you both get the maximum benefit from the session. This is also something they can hold on to, or have up on their wall, either in the days leading up to your session, or at the meeting itself, to remind them what they can expect and what is coming next.

#31

STICK TO THE PLAN

Now, it might seem like this point is being driven home a lot, but it is well worth going over – not just why you should stick to the plan, but also the impact it can have if you do not. Anyone with autism will know full well how hard it can be when plans are changed on short notice. Autistic people tend to hold the view that plans are there to be adhered to, and there is no point making plans if you're then going to change them. Even a small change to the plan at short notice can make us feel unwell, sick to the stomach, or overwhelmed and confused. We can start to panic, and find it hard to keep up with anything that is being said. Becoming overloaded or overwhelmed has been described as a feeling of falling out of reality. That might sound like a strange way to describe it, but unless you have felt it, then it's hard to understand. It feels as if your thoughts grow slow and cannot be put in any kind of real order – everything that everyone else says seems to be too complex to understand. Noises, however small, are hard to bear, and in that moment, the autistic person is completely incapable of making any decisions or plans. This is not always brought on by changes to plans, but that can be something that leads to it, or can be a contributing factor. It goes without saying that this is best avoided, not just for autistic people, but also for yourself, as you don't get the most out of us when we are in that state. Sometimes a small change can trigger this, but the truth is that it is most likely just part of a longer build up that might have gone unnoticed. However, the point is, that even something that seems small and easy might lead to these kinds of feelings, and a wasted meeting!

#32

ASK SPECIFIC RATHER THAN OPEN-ENDED QUESTIONS

There is a huge difference between asking someone 'How do you find travelling on public transport?', them saying 'Fine' and you thinking that's that, and asking them a longer list of questions and probing deeper. Someone with autism might find it hard to offer up information without being asked for it specifically, so them saying they are fine to travel might not tell you that there is only one trip they can take on their own, or that they have to have someone meet them or they cannot take the bus. It does not tell you what they do, or how they cope if their bus or train is late or cancelled. Asking follow-up questions, and more importantly, specific follow-up questions, will get you a lot more important information. For example, with an autistic person who finds travelling okay, but only because of the specific way they travel, finding out more about this is key. Most people would be able to understand that they need to volunteer that extra information, but that is not something all autistic people will be able to do, so you might ask questions such as the ones below.

'When was the last time you were on a bus?' 'And did you have anyone with you then, or did you go and get it by yourself?' 'And did anyone meet you when you got off the bus?' Then you could ask 'How did you feel doing this?' but again maybe break that down: ask if they felt stressed, or upset or if they felt relaxed. You could ask things like 'Has your bus ever broken down? If so, how did you find having to go and get another one?' 'What do you do if you miss your bus?' 'If you're out and about, and you realise you don't have change for the bus, what do you do?' I know that it seems like a lot, but just think about how much more information you are getting – you no longer see half the picture, instead you see and know everything you need to know. And yes, it is a lot, and yes, it might take a long time. I am sure the people you are talking to might get a bit annoyed at times with you asking so much, the same as you might get a bit fed up with having to ask – there is nothing wrong with that. An open-ended question is something autistic people tend to hate; it means there is a good chance that they might miss something out, or say something that sounds right in their head, but does not fit what is being asked. Going for details, and asking specific questions will take longer, but it will help in the long run.

#33

······························

PACE YOUR SPEECH

Be aware of how fast you are talking. People with autism often find it hard to follow what you are saying if you are talking too fast. This is nothing to do with them not understanding the concept of what you are talking about, but rather it is due to them needing some time to process what has been said. It takes longer for people with autism to process information, so if it comes too fast we miss bits of it while we are busy processing what has already been said. Take a break every so often, and check that whomever you are talking to is keeping up. If they aren't, go back over what you have said, and slow down from that point on. You might not think you are talking that fast, but it might still be hard to follow for the person you are talking to – you need to be guided by them, not by how you feel. If you do talk too fast, the chances are that whomever you are talking to will miss what you are saying, and you will waste time having to go over it. It's much better just to slow yourself down the first time you are telling them. Talking too fast or too loud, or for too long can bring on overload in the autistic person you are talking to. I know it seems like a lot to keep track of, but the key is to say only what needs to be said and then stop. Fast talking often makes autistic people feel confused, again, not because they don't understand the words, but because they can't process what is being said to them.

It's about remembering that someone with autism might look as if they are taking in everything you are saying on the outside, but they might be completely overwhelmed on the inside and not be hearing any of it. So taking a break every now and then to make sure you are not talking too fast is important. When you become excited or overenthusiastic about something, it is easy and even natural to start talking faster, but that is something you will have to try to control. If you are overstressed or worried about time, this can also be an issue, but talking fast can have an impact on how well someone with autism understands you, and therefore you end up wasting even more time having to go back and explain!

#34

....

ALTERNATIVES
TO NON-VERBAL
COMMUNICATION

If someone is not understanding your non-verbal communication (NVC), what can you do to help them with this? Bear in mind that helping them might not mean teaching them to understand NVC, but just giving them something they can use in its place while the two of you talk, to help them to get on. This does not mean you have given up on them ever understanding NVC, but it means that you are giving them a way to communicate that is non-verbal to get them started. NVC is a huge part of how most people communicate, and as addressed before in this book, it's impossible to deny that autistic people do miss out by not being able to follow it.

Talking can be hard for people with autism, and we might find it hard to say how we feel about certain things, ask for a break or say when we are starting to feel overwhelmed. Therefore, practical NVC is something that could be helpful for autistics. One good way of doing this would be with signs. That way the autistic person can just hold up a sign saying they feel overwhelmed, or need a break. They do not have to rely on body language to communicate this, and if they are finding it hard to talk, a sign might be the perfect way to communicate with you.

You might use sketches to communicate an idea to an autistic person. So you would draw an image of what it was you were trying to say, to help yourself be understood. This small visual aid can sometimes make all the difference to someone with autism, and their understanding of what it is you are trying to communicate to them.

Another thing that you have to bear in mind is that autistic people might not understand your gestures. So if you shrug your shoulders be sure also to say 'I don't know'. Don't assume that the person you are talking to is going to understand the meaning of your gesture. Just speaking at the same time as gesturing or showing the autistic person a visual aid to back up your meaning can not only help them to understand what you mean in the moment, but might also help them to understand what that gesture means in the future.

#35

....

THINGS TO CONSIDER WHEN OFFERING FOOD

It is well known that autistic people can have a lot of issues around food. There might be allergies, or someone might feel they can only eat certain foods or a particular brand. Or someone with autism might be routined and need to eat their meals at the same time each day. So, with this in mind, what should be done about offering autistic people food during meetings, appointments or workshops?

The first thing is to think about what time the meeting will be, and how long it will run for. Then talk to people. It might be a case of asking someone if they have any dietary requirements in advance, and then making sure that if food is being offered it is something they can have. It is not very fair to provide food only for it to turn out that the autistic person cannot eat it. Those requirements might be because of allergies, or they might be down to someone feeling that they can eat only certain things, but whatever it is, a quick question when setting up the meeting can deal with it.

It is not as if people are going to be eating all the time in meetings, but putting in a bit of planning never hurts. Also, if the meeting is at someone's house, and their routine dictates that they need to eat when the meeting is taking place, that should be fine. Stopping them from doing so will only disrupt their routine, and stress them out even more than the meeting itself. If you can avoid being there at meal times, that would be better.

Eating during a meeting might not be a conmon thing, but there is nothing wrong with it. Long sessions will need breaks, and that might be a more appropriate time to eat, but it is important to include everyone in this, and to make sure that if offering food it is something the autistic person will be able to eat.

CONCLUSION

This book was written with the intention of giving a few easy-to-follow and important tips on autism and the use of language to professionals working with autistic people – and hopefully it has done this. The main focus of the book was, of course, language, and the use of language, and I am sure you agree with me when I say that this is a complex and wide ranging topic. As I said at the start of this book, as a young autistic man I have met a lot of professionals over the years – some have been good, some great and some just awful – but one thing that is important to take away from this book would be that I am not saying you are bad if you do not already do all of the things I recommend in this book. No one knows everything, and everyone can always learn something new. There is no shame in trying out new things and trying to improve in your work, even if you have been doing your job for years there is still room for you to experiment with new ways of doing things. I don't claim to know everything there is to know about working with autistic people, but what I can tell you is that I know what it's like to be someone who is autistic dealing with you. I know how helpful all of the things in this book can be as I have experienced first-hand people who do them, and people who don't. All I can say is that I hope you don't feel this book has been too harsh on professionals – it's not about putting anyone down for not working in a certain way, it's about helping autism professionals to think about things they might not have thought of, and to improve their relationships with the autistic people they work with.

Lastly, I want to say that I hope you have found at least something in this book helpful; it might be that you already knew and applied 34 out of the 35 tips in this book, but even if this is the case, at least you found something new in here that might be helpful in your working relationship with autistic people in the future.

of related interest

Autism Equality in the Workplace
Removing Barriers and Challenging Discrimination
Janine Booth
Foreword by John McDonnell MP
ISBN 978 1 84905 678 6
eISBN 978 1 78450 197 6

The Essential Manual for Asperger Syndrome (ASD) in the Classroom
What Every Teacher Needs to Know
Kathy Hoopmann Illustrated by Rebecca Houkamau
ISBN 978 1 84905 553 6
eISBN 978 0 85700 984 5

Teaching University Students with Autism Spectrum Disorder
A Guide to Developing Academic Capacity and Proficiency
Kimberley McMahon-Coleman and Kim Draisma
ISBN 978 1 84905 420 1
eISBN 978 0 85700 798 8

Counselling People on the Autism Spectrum
A Practical Manual
Katherine Paxton and Irene A. Estay
ISBN 978 1 84310 552 7
eISBN 978 1 84642 627 8

Helping Children with Autism Spectrum Conditions through Everyday Transitions
Small Changes – Big Challenges
John Smith, Jane Donlan and Bob Smith
ISBN 978 1 84905 275 7
eISBN 978 0 85700 572 4